DEDIC

TO MY LORD AND SAVIOR, JESUS CHRIST:

YOU ARE THE AUTHOR AND PERFECTER OF MY FAITH, THE ONE WHO HAS GUIDED ME THROUGH EVERY VALLEY AND MOUNTAINTOP. THIS WORK IS FIRST AND FOREMOST DEDICATED TO YOU.

THANK YOU FOR YOUR UNFAILING LOVE, YOUR ENDLESS GRACE, AND YOUR CONSTANT PRESENCE IN MY LIFE. EVERY WORD HERE IS A TESTAMENT TO YOUR FAITHFULNESS AND THE HOPE YOU'VE INSTILLED IN ME THROUGH EACH SEASON OF MY JOURNEY. MAY THESE PAGES REFLECT YOUR HEART AND DRAW OTHERS CLOSER TO YOU.

TO MY BELOVED WIFE, DINA:

YOU HAVE BEEN MY STEADFAST COMPANION, MY UNWAVERING SUPPORT, AND MY GREATEST EARTHLY BLESSING. THROUGH CAREER CHANGES, HEALTH CHALLENGES, AND EVERY TWIST AND TURN OF OUR JOURNEY TOGETHER, YOU'VE STOOD BY ME WITH LOVE, PATIENCE, AND UNWAVERING FAITH. YOUR STRENGTH HAS LIFTED ME IN MY WEAKEST MOMENTS, AND YOUR JOY HAS BRIGHTENED MY DARKEST DAYS.

THIS BOOK IS AS MUCH A PRODUCT OF YOUR LOVE AND ENCOURAGEMENT AS IT IS OF MY EXPERIENCES. THANK YOU FOR BELIEVING IN ME, FOR PRAYING WITH ME AND FOR ME, AND FOR HELPING ME SEE GOD'S HAND AT WORK IN EVERY CIRCUMSTANCE.

YOUR LOVE IS A DAILY REMINDER OF GOD'S GRACE IN MY LIFE.
MAY THIS DEVOTIONAL BE A BLESSING TO ALL WHO READ IT, JUST AS YOU BOTH HAVE BEEN AN IMMEASURABLE BLESSING TO ME.

WITH ALL MY LOVE AND GRATITUDE,
DOUG

INTRODUCTION

Life has a way of throwing curveballs when we least expect it. One moment, we may feel like we're on top of the world, with everything going according to plan. The next, we find ourselves facing uncertainty, financial struggles, difficult decisions, or heartbreaking loss. In these moments, it's easy to feel like our world is crumbling beneath our feet, and we may wonder where God is in the midst of it all.

But what if these challenges are actually invitations to a deeper faith and trust in God? What if, instead of seeing these trials as obstacles to our happiness, we viewed them as opportunities to experience God's faithfulness, provision, and redemptive purposes in new ways?

Over the next four weeks, we'll explore what it means to trust God in the midst of life's storms. Each week, we'll dive into a different area of struggle - uncertainty, financial strain, decision-making, and loss - and discover how God meets us in these places with His unchanging character, unfailing love, and transformative grace.
Through daily reflections, scripture meditations, and practical action steps, we'll learn how to:

Find unshakeable peace and security in God's sovereignty, even when the future feels uncertain.

Experience God's provision and sufficiency in times of financial hardship and lack.

Seek God's wisdom and direction when faced with difficult decisions and crossroads.

Cling to hope in God's redemptive purposes, even in the face of devastating loss and disappointment.

Along the way, we'll draw encouragement and insight from the stories of biblical heroes who navigated their own storms with faith and trust in God. We'll discover that our struggles are not unique, and that God is always faithful to see His children through the toughest of times.

.

INTRODUCTION

Whether you're currently in the midst of a storm or simply want to strengthen your faith for the challenges ahead, this devotional journey is for you

As we fix our eyes on Jesus and anchor our hope in His promises, may we find the courage and strength to trust God in every season of life, knowing that He is always good and always faithful.

So let's dive in, expectant that God will meet us in the pages ahead and transform our hearts and minds as we learn to trust Him more deeply.

"Let us hold unswervingly to the hope we profess, for he who promised is faithful." - Hebrews 10:23 NIV

PREFACE

DEAR FELLOW SOJOURNER,

IF YOU'VE PICKED UP THIS DEVOTIONAL, CHANCES ARE YOU'RE NAVIGATING SOME
CHALLENGING CIRCUMSTANCES. WHETHER YOU'RE FACING UNCERTAINTY,
FINANCIAL STRUGGLES, DIFFICULT DECISIONS, OR DEVASTATING LOSS, I WANT YOU
TO KNOW THAT YOU'RE NOT ALONE, AND THAT THERE IS HOPE TO BE FOUND IN
THE PAGES AHEAD.

I'VE WALKED THROUGH MY OWN SHARE OF TRIALS, AND I KNOW FIRSTHAND
HOW EASY IT IS TO FEEL OVERWHELMED AND EVEN ABANDONED BY GOD IN THE
MIDST OF LIFE'S STORMS. BUT IN THE DARKEST OF VALLEYS, I'VE ALSO
EXPERIENCED HIS UNSHAKEABLE FAITHFULNESS, TENDER COMPASSION, AND
TRANSFORMATIVE POWER. TIME AND TIME AGAIN, HE HAS MET ME IN MY
WEAKNESS AND GIVEN ME THE GRACE TO TRUST HIM MORE DEEPLY.

OVER THE NEXT FOUR WEEKS, WE'LL EXPLORE WHAT IT MEANS TO TRUST GOD
IN THE FACE OF LIFE'S CHALLENGES. WE'LL DIVE INTO SCRIPTURE, ENGAGE IN
HONEST REFLECTION, AND TAKE PRACTICAL STEPS TO DEEPEN OUR FAITH AND
DEPENDENCE ON GOD. ALONG THE WAY, I'LL SHARE SOME OF MY OWN INSIGHTS,
NOT AS SOMEONE WHO HAS IT ALL FIGURED OUT, BUT AS A FELLOW TRAVELER
ON THIS JOURNEY OF FAITH.

BUT MORE THAN ANYTHING, I WANT TO INVITE YOU TO HEAR FROM GOD HIMSELF
IN THESE PAGES. HE IS THE TRUE AUTHOR AND PERFECTER OF OUR FAITH, AND
HIS SPIRIT IS READY TO SPEAK, COMFORT, AND GUIDE YOU. SO BE EXPECTANT,
LISTEN FOR HIS VOICE, AND LEAN INTO HIS UNFAILING LOVE AND GRACE.

MY FRIEND, THERE IS HOPE, PURPOSE, AND VICTORY ON THE OTHER SIDE OF THIS
STORM. OUR GOD IS FAITHFUL, AND HE WILL USE EVERY STRUGGLE FOR YOUR
GOOD AND HIS GLORY. SO TAKE HEART, FIX YOUR EYES ON JESUS, AND LET'S
TRUST GOD TOGETHER, KNOWING THAT HIS MERCY IS NEW EVERY MORNING AND
HIS LOVE NEVER FAILS.

HOLDING THE LIGHT FOR YOU ON THIS JOURNEY,
DOUG HAMILTON

WEEK 1
EMBRACING BROKENNESS
FINDING GOD'S STRENGTH IN OUR WEAKEST MOMENTS

Key Verse: *"The Lord is near to the brokenhearted and saves the crushed in spirit."* - Psalm 34:18 ESV

Life has a way of shattering our expectations, doesn't it? I've experienced this firsthand throughout my journey. From swinging hammers in construction to owning my own business, to computer animation (my favorite job), and now as a Christian counselor and pastor (my most fulfilling) - each transition brought its own set of broken dreams and shattered illusions.

There were times when I felt like a walking jigsaw puzzle, pieces scattered across a lifetime of career changes and personal struggles. Depression and anxiety were unwelcome companions, breaking down the walls of self-reliance I had so carefully constructed. Three nervous breakdowns later, I found myself facing a hard truth: I was utterly and completely broken.

But here's the beautiful paradox of our faith: it's in our brokenness that we often encounter God most profoundly. When our perfectly curated life plans lie in pieces at our feet, that's when we're most open to the gentle hands of the Master Potter.

In my darkest moments, when I felt most shattered, I discovered a God who doesn't shy away from our brokenness. Instead, He draws near. He doesn't demand that we pull ourselves together before approaching Him. He meets us in the midst of our mess, offering comfort, hope, and the promise of restoration.

But God doesn't just comfort us in our brokenness; He uses it. Every shattered piece becomes raw material in His hands. The career setbacks that left me questioning my worth? They became stepping stones to a calling I never could have imagined. The mental health struggles that made me feel weak and inadequate? They became a source of empathy and connection with others facing similar battles.

SHATTERED PIECES

Reflect and Respond:

- What areas of your life feel shattered or broken right now?
- How have you typically responded to brokenness in the past? With denial, anger, or surrender?
- Can you recall a time when you experienced God's nearness in a moment of brokenness?

Action Steps:

1. Take some time to honestly pour out your heart to God. Name the broken pieces of your life, knowing He can handle your raw emotions.
2. Read Psalm 34 slowly, paying special attention to verse 18. How does it comfort you to know that God is near to the brokenhearted?
3. Share your experience of brokenness with a trusted friend or counselor. Remember, we weren't meant to pick up the pieces alone.

Remember, embracing brokenness isn't about staying broken. It's about allowing God to put us back together in His way, for His purposes. And in that process, we often discover a strength, beauty, and purpose we never knew was possible.

"God uses broken things. It takes broken soil to produce a crop, broken clouds to give rain, broken grain to give bread, broken bread to give strength. It is the broken alabaster box that gives forth perfume." - Vance Havner

My Notes

_____

_____

_____

SURRENDER'S HEALING

Key Verse: *"Come to me, all you who are weary and burdened, and I will give you rest."* - Matthew 11:28 NIV

Surrender. It's not a word we typically associate with strength or healing. In our culture, we're taught to fight, to push through, to never give up. But what if true healing begins when we finally stop struggling and surrender?

I remember the day I finally surrendered my career ambitions to God. After years of jumping from job to job, always searching for that perfect fit, I found myself at the end of my rope. I was exhausted, disillusioned, and frankly, scared. What if I never found my true calling? What if all these career changes were just a waste of time?

It was in that moment of desperation that I heard God's gentle invitation: "Come to me. Lay down your burdens. Rest in me." At first, I resisted. Surely, I just needed to try harder, make a better plan, network more effectively. But the more I fought, the more weary I became.

It was at the moment of my surrender the I began my healing journey. It didn't immediately solve all my problems or magically reveal my life's purpose. But it did something even more profound: it shifted my perspective. Instead of seeing my worth through the lens of my career achievements, I began to see myself as God sees me - beloved, valuable, with a purpose beyond my job title.

This doesn't mean the healing process was easy or quick. There were still difficult days, moments of doubt, and times when I was tempted to take back control. But each time I surrendered anew, I experienced a deeper level of God's peace and healing.

Surrender's healing is paradoxical. In letting go, we gain. In admitting our weakness, we find strength. In acknowledging our brokenness, we open ourselves to God's restoration. It's not a one-time event, but a daily choice to trust God with every aspect of our lives.

SURRENDER'S HEALING

As you face your own broken places today, I invite you to consider: what do you need to surrender? What burdens are you carrying that were never meant for you to bear alone? Remember, God's invitation is always open: "Come to me, all you who are weary and burdened, and I will give you rest."

Reflect and Respond:

- What areas of your life do you find hardest to surrender to God? Why?
- How have you experienced God's rest or healing through surrender in the past?
- What might be holding you back from fully surrendering to God right now?

Action Steps:

1. Create a physical reminder of your surrender. This could be tying a ribbon around a tree, placing a stone in a special spot, or creating a piece of art.
2. Practice surrender through breath prayer. As you inhale, silently pray "I surrender"; as you exhale, pray "to You, Lord."
3. Share your decision to surrender with a trusted friend or mentor. Ask them to pray for you and hold you accountable.

Remember, surrender isn't about giving up. It's about exchanging our limited strength for God's limitless power. It's in this place of surrender that we often find the deepest healing and the truest rest for our souls.

"Surrender to what is. Let go of what was. Have faith in what will be." - Sonia Ricotti

Key Verse: "And we know that for those who love God all things work together for good, for those who are called according to his purpose." - Romans 8:28 ESV

I used to think that brokenness was the end of the story. After all, who wants a shattered vase or a cracked mirror? But God, in His infinite wisdom and creativity, sees beauty where we see only brokenness.

During one particularly dark period of depression, I couldn't imagine how anything good could come from the mess I was in. My career was in shambles, my self-worth at rock bottom. But it was in that very darkness that God began to paint with light.

He took my experiences of brokenness and began to use them to help others. My struggles with mental health became a bridge of empathy to those battling similar demons. My career failures became testimonies of God's faithfulness and provision.

Like a master artist creating a mosaic, God doesn't waste a single broken piece of our lives. He uses every shard, every fragment, to create something beautiful - often more stunning than we could have imagined in our unbroken state.

This process of beauty emerging from brokenness isn't always quick or painless. Sometimes, it feels like we're being broken even further as God reshapes us. But just as a sculptor must chip away at a block of marble to reveal the masterpiece within, God often uses our broken places to sculpt us into the image of Christ.

I've seen this in my own life, time and time again. The very things that once caused me shame or regret have become the cornerstone of my ministry. The depression that once threatened to destroy me now allows me to speak hope into the lives of others who are struggling. The career setbacks that seemed like failures have become stepping stones to a calling I never could have imagined.

BEAUTY'S EMERGENCE

This doesn't mean we should seek out brokenness or glorify suffering. But it does mean that when brokenness finds us - as it inevitably will in this fallen world - we can trust that God is at work, creating beauty even in the midst of pain.

Reflect and Respond:

- Where have you seen beauty emerge from brokenness in your own life?
- How might God be using your current struggles to create something?
- In what ways has your brokenness allowed you to connect with or help others?

Action Steps:

1. Create or find an image that represents beauty emerging from brokenness (like a flower growing through concrete). Use it as a visual reminder of God's restorative work.
2. Share your story of God's redemptive work with someone who's struggling. Your emergence from brokenness could be the hope they need.
3. Meditate on Romans 8:28. How might this promise change your perspective on your current challenges?

Remember, in God's economy, nothing is wasted. Every broken piece, every painful experience, every setback can be used by Him to create something beautiful. Trust the Artist's hand, even when you can't yet see the masterpiece He's creating.

"The world breaks everyone and afterward many are strong at the broken places." - Ernest Hemingway

STRENGTH'S FOUNDATION

Key Verse: *"But he said to me, 'My grace is sufficient for you, for my power is made perfect in weakness.' Therefore I will boast all the more gladly of my weaknesses, so that the power of Christ may rest upon me." - 2 Corinthians 12:9 ESV*

If you're anything like me, you've probably bought into the world's definition of strength at some point. I know I did. I thought strength meant having it all together, never showing vulnerability, always being the one with the answers. Boy, was I wrong.

It took multiple career changes, bouts of depression, and yes, even those three nervous breakdowns, for me to realize that true strength isn't about never falling down. It's about how we get back up - and more importantly, Who we lean on in the process.

Paul's words in 2 Corinthians 12:9 used to baffle me. Boast in weaknesses? That seemed counterintuitive. But I've come to understand that our weaknesses, our broken places, are precisely where God's strength shines through most brightly.

When we're at our weakest, that's when we're most open to relying on God's strength. And let me tell you, His strength is a much more reliable foundation than any we could build on our own.

I remember a time when I was struggling with severe anxiety. I felt weak, ashamed, and utterly incapable of fulfilling my roles as a counselor and pastor. How could I help others when I could barely help myself? But it was in that place of weakness that I experienced God's strength in a profound way.

STRENGTHENING YOURSELF

As I learned to lean on Him, to admit my need for His grace, I found a strength that went beyond my own capabilities. I discovered that my weakness didn't disqualify me from ministry – it actually made me more effective. My struggles allowed me to connect with others in their pain, to offer genuine empathy rather than pat answers.

This doesn't mean we should seek out weakness or avoid growing stronger. But it does mean that we can embrace our limitations, knowing that they create space for God's power to be displayed in our lives.

Reflect and Respond:

- How has God's strength shown up in your moments of weakness?
- In what areas of your life do you need to rely more on God's strength rather than your own?
- How might your weaknesses actually be opportunities for God's power to be displayed?

Action Steps:

1. Write down three of your perceived weaknesses. Then, pray over each one, asking God to show you how His strength can be perfected in these areas.
2. Memorize 2 Corinthians 12:9. Recite it to yourself whenever you feel weak or inadequate.
3. Practice vulnerability by admitting a struggle to a trusted friend or mentor. Allow them to support and pray for you.

Remember, true strength isn't found in having it all together, but in knowing the One who holds all things together.

"God does not give us overcoming life: He gives us life as we overcome." – Oswald Chambers

GRACE'S SUFFICIENCY

Key Verse: "And God is able to make all grace abound to you, so that having all sufficiency in all things at all times, you may abound in every good work." - 2 Corinthians 9:8 ESV

Grace. It's a word we use often in Christian circles, but do we really understand its power? I know I didn't for a long time. I thought grace was just about forgiveness, about God overlooking my sins. But I've come to realize it's so much more than that.

Grace is the fuel that powers our journey through brokenness to wholeness. It's the gentle hand that picks us up when we fall, the strength that sustains us when our own reserves are depleted, the love that embraces us in our messiest moments.

I remember a time when I felt completely insufficient. I was facing challenges in my ministry that seemed far beyond my capabilities. The weight of others' expectations, combined with my own self-doubt, left me feeling crushed. It was in that place of insufficiency that I truly began to understand the sufficiency of God's grace.

You see, grace isn't just about covering our past mistakes. It's about empowering us for present challenges and future calling. It's the divine enablement that allows us to do what we could never do on our own.

In my moment of weakness, I experienced grace as a tangible force. It wasn't just a concept; it was the very presence of God, filling me, strengthening me, enabling me to move forward when I thought I couldn't take another step.

This grace doesn't demand that we have it all together. In fact, it often shows up most powerfully in our places of lack. When we're not enough, His grace is sufficient. When we're overwhelmed, His grace abounds. When we feel disqualified, His grace qualifies us.

WEEK 1 DAY 5 OF OUR JOURNEY
GRACE'S SUFFICIENCY

Remember, God's grace isn't rationed out in small portions. It abounds. It overflows. It's more than enough for whatever you're facing today. Rest in its sufficiency, draw strength from its power, and watch how it transforms your perspective on your brokenness and challenges.

Reflect and Respond:

- How have you experienced God's grace in your life recently?
- In what areas do you need to more fully embrace God's grace?
- How might your view of yourself and your challenges change if you truly believed in the sufficiency of God's grace?

Action Steps:

1. Write a "grace list" – note down specific ways you've experienced God's grace, both in big moments and small daily mercies.
2. Practice extending grace to yourself. When you make a mistake or fall short, remind yourself of God's abundant grace.
3. Look for opportunities to extend grace to others today. How can you be a channel of God's grace in your relationships?

"Grace is not simply leniency when we have sinned. Grace is the enabling gift of God not to sin. Grace is power, not just pardon."
- John Piper

POTTER'S HANDS

Key Verse: *"We can make our plans, but the Lord determines our steps."* - Proverbs 16:9 NLT

You know, there's something deeply humbling about realizing you're clay in the Potter's hands. After decades of trying to mold my own life - jumping from construction to stage performer to computer animation, to owning my own company always searching for that elusive sense of purpose and worth- I finally had to admit that I wasn't the master craftsman I thought I was.

It's funny how God works. He took all those seemingly disjointed pieces of my life - the career changes, the bouts of depression, even my tendency to talk too much - and started shaping them into something I never could have imagined on my own.

Being clay isn't always comfortable. Sometimes the Potter's hands feel like they're squeezing too hard or reshaping parts of us we'd rather leave alone. But here's the beautiful thing: He sees the masterpiece when we can only feel the pressure.

I remember a particularly difficult season when it felt like God was allowing the dismantling of the life I had built. My career was in flux, my mental health was fragile, and I couldn't see any rhyme or reason to what was happening. It was as if the Potter had thrown me back onto the wheel and was starting over from scratch.

But as I got tired of fighting and surrendered to His shaping hands, I began to see glimpses of the vessel He was creating. My diverse work experiences became a unique perspective to bring to ministry. My struggles with mental health became a wellspring of empathy for others facing similar battles.

Even my false extroverted nature, which I often saw as a weakness, became a strength in connecting with people and sharing God's love.

POTTER'S HANDS

The process of being shaped by God is ongoing. There are still days when I resist His touch, when I want to jump off the potter's wheel and shape myself. But I'm learning to trust the Potter's hands, knowing that He sees the finished product even when I can't.

Reflect and Respond:

- In what areas of your life do you feel God's hands actively shaping you right now?
- How has your view of God as the Potter changed over time?
- What parts of your life feel 'misshapen' or useless? How might God be using even these for His purposes?

Action Steps:

1. Spend some time in prayer, consciously placing yourself in God's hands. Be specific about areas where you need His shaping touch.
2. Write a letter to your younger self, explaining how God has used even the "messy" parts of your journey for His purposes.
3. If possible, try your hand at actual pottery or clay work. As you shape the clay, reflect on how God shapes us with even greater care and skill.

Remember, friends, no matter how many times we've cracked or crumbled, the Potter isn't finished with us yet. He's still molding us into vessels fit for His purposes - and sometimes, the cracks are exactly where His light shines through the brightest.

"We are all broken. That's how the light gets in." - Ernest Hemingway

RESTORATION'S PROMISE

Key Verse: *"And the God of all grace, who called you to his eternal glory in Christ, after you have suffered a little while, will himself restore you and make you strong, firm and steadfast." - 1 Peter 5:10 NIV*

Well, folks, we've come to the end of our first week together, and if you're anything like me, you might be feeling a bit raw. Embracing brokenness isn't exactly a walk in the park, is it? But here's the good news - it's not the end of the story.

I remember a time when I thought my third nervous breakdown was going to be the final nail in the coffin of my usefulness to God. I mean, what kind of counselor or pastor has more breakdowns than career changes, right? (And trust me, I had a lot of career changes!) But that's when God's promise of restoration became more than just a nice Bible verse to me.

Restoration doesn't always look like we expect. Sometimes, God doesn't just patch up our old dreams; He gives us entirely new ones. He takes our brokenness and creates a mosaic more beautiful than we could have imagined. For me, that looked like using my experiences with mental health struggles to connect with and help others facing similar battles.

The journey of restoration is rarely quick or easy. It often involves pain, uncertainty, and moments where we wonder if we'll ever feel whole again. But God's promise is sure. He is in the business of restoration, and He's incredibly good at His job.

I've seen this play out in my own life time and time again. The career setbacks that once left me feeling like a failure became the very experiences God used to guide me into my true calling. The mental health struggles that made me feel weak and disqualified became the source of my greatest ministry opportunities.

RESTORATION'S PROMISE

God's restoration doesn't just return us to our former state - it often leaves us stronger, more compassionate, and better equipped for the purposes He has for us.

Reflect and Respond:

- Where do you need to trust God's promise of restoration in your life right now?
- How have you seen God's restorative work in your past? How might that encourage you for the future?
- In what ways might God be using your current brokenness to prepare you for future purposes?

Action Steps:

1. Make a "restoration playlist" of songs that remind you of God's faithfulness and His promise to make all things new.
2. Reach out to someone who has been through a similar struggle to yours and is further along in their journey. Ask them to share how they've experienced God's restoration.
3. Choose a "restoration verse" (like our key verse or another that speaks to you) to memorize and meditate on in the coming week.

As we close this week, remember that embracing brokenness isn't about staying broken - it's about allowing God to put us back together in His way and for His purposes. And let me tell you, His restoration work is something to behold. After all, He's in the business of making beauty from ashes, and friends, that's a business that never goes under.

"God is not helpless among the ruins. God's strength is made perfect in our weakness. And His strength is made beautiful in the ruins." - John Piper

My Notes

Dear Friend,

As we close this week on embracing brokenness, I hope you've begun to see your broken places in a new light. Remember, God doesn't discard the broken - He treasures it. Your cracks and imperfections are the very spaces where His light can shine through most brilliantly.

In the coming week, I encourage you to look at your struggles not as setbacks, but as opportunities for God's transformative work. Be gentle with yourself, knowing that healing is a process. And don't be afraid to let others see your brokenness - it might be exactly what someone else needs to find hope in their own journey.

May you find comfort in knowing that the God who created the universe is intimately involved in putting your broken pieces back together, creating something even more beautiful than before.

With hope and encouragement, Doug

"REFINING FIRE: FORGING UNSHAKEABLE FAITH THROUGH LIFE'S CHALLENGES"

FAITH'S CRUCIBLE

Key Verse: *"These have come so that the proven genuineness of your faith—of greater worth than gold, which perishes even though refined by fire—may result in praise, glory and honor when Jesus Christ is revealed."* - 1 Peter 1:7 NIV

Have you ever watched a goldsmith at work? It's a fascinating process. The craftsman subjects the gold to intense heat, causing impurities to rise to the surface where they can be removed. This refining process is repeated until the gold is pure, with the goldsmith able to see his reflection in the molten metal.

In many ways, our faith journey mirrors this refining process. Life has a way of turning up the heat, doesn't it? Whether it's career setbacks, health challenges, or relationship struggles, these trials can feel like a crucible, testing the very core of our beliefs.

I remember when I had attempted to have a successful career in technology, A small computer company I was trying to get started with some partners, only to see it crumble during an a health scare.

Everything I had worked for seemed to go up in smoke overnight. My faith, once strong and unwavering, was suddenly put to the test. Would I trust God in the face of financial uncertainty? Could I find purpose beyond my professional identity?

As the heat of his circumstances intensified, impurities in my faith began to surface. I realized how much I had relied on my own abilities rather than God's provision. My fear of failure and need for control became glaringly apparent. It was uncomfortable, even painful at times, but this refining process was revealing the true nature of my faith.

Through this crucible experience, something beautiful began to emerge. As I surrendered my plans and fears to God, my faith became more genuine and more resilient.

FAITH'S CRUCIBLE

I was beginning to discover a strength that went beyond my professional capabilities—a strength rooted in my identity as a child of God.

The refining fire didn't just restore my former faith; it transformed it into something far more precious. I emerged with a faith that was tested, proven, and more valuable than any worldly success.

Reflect and Respond:

- What "crucible moments" have you experienced in your faith journey?
- How has your faith been tested recently? What has this process revealed about your relationship with God?
- In what ways has God used challenging circumstances to refine and strengthen your faith?

Action Steps:

1. Identify a current challenge you're facing. Pray for God to use this as an opportunity to refine and strengthen your faith.
2. Write down three "impurities" in your faith that surface during difficult times (e.g., doubt, self-reliance, fear). Ask God to help you surrender these to Him.
3. Share with a trusted friend or small group about a time when your faith was tested. How did you see God work through that situation?

Remember, the refiner's fire isn't meant to destroy us—it's meant to purify us. Just as gold becomes more valuable through the refining process, our faith becomes more precious as it's tested and proven genuine.

"Count it all joy, my brothers, when you meet trials of various kinds, for you know that the testing of your faith produces steadfastness." - James 1:2-3 ESV

SOVEREIGN FLAMES

Key Verse: : *"And we know that in all things God works for the good of those who love him, who have been called according to his purpose." - Romans 8:28 NIV*

Have you ever found yourself in the midst of a fiery trial, wondering if God has somehow lost control? I've been there, and let me tell you, it's a lonely and frightening place to be. But what if I told you that even in the hottest flames, God remains sovereign?

This reminds me of Joseph in the Bible. His story is a powerful testament to God's sovereignty in the midst of seemingly hopeless situations. Sold into slavery by his own brothers, falsely accused and imprisoned in Egypt, Joseph had every reason to question God's plan.

From the outside, it looked like Joseph's world was crumbling. He lost his family, his freedom, and his reputation. In his darkest moments, he might have wondered, "How could any good come from this?"

But as Joseph clung to his faith, he began to see glimpses of God's sovereign hand at work. His time as a slave in Potiphar's house and his years in prison honed his leadership skills. His ability to interpret dreams, a gift from God, eventually brought him before Pharaoh.

In the end, the very trials that seemed to destroy Joseph's life positioned him to become second-in-command over all of Egypt. He was able to save not only the Egyptians from famine but also his own family - the very brothers who had sold him into slavery.

Years later, Joseph could confidently tell his brothers, "You intended to harm me, but God intended it for good to accomplish what is now being done, the saving of many lives" (Genesis 50:20).

SOVEREIGN FLAMES

You see, God's sovereignty doesn't mean we won't face fires in this life. But it does mean that He remains in control even when the flames are at their hottest. He uses these fires not to destroy us, but to refine us, to shape us more into the image of Christ.

Reflect and Respond:

- Can you recall a time when something that seemed disastrous actually worked out for your good?
- How does remembering God's sovereignty change your perspective on current challenges?
- In what areas of your life do you need to trust God's sovereign control right now?

Action Steps:

1. Make a list of three difficult situations you're facing. Next to each, write "God is sovereign" as a reminder of His control.
2. Spend time in prayer, surrendering your current struggles to God's sovereign care. Be specific about areas where you need to trust Him more.
3. Share with someone how you've seen God work good out of a challenging situation in your past. Encourage them to look for God's sovereign hand in their own trials.

Remember, friends, even when life feels like a dumpster fire, God remains on the throne. He is working all things - yes, even the painful, fiery things - for the good of those who love Him. Trust in His sovereign flames; they're refining you for a purpose beyond what you can see right now.

"God's sovereignty is not so much a theological doctrine as a place of rest." - Charles Spurgeon

GOODNESS PREVAILS

Key Verse: *"The Lord is good, a refuge in times of trouble. He cares for those who trust in him."* – Nahum 1:7 NIV

Let me tell you, friends, when you've hopped from career to career like I have, it's easy to question whether you're on the right path. Add in struggles with depression and anxiety, and you've got a recipe for doubt. But here's what I've learned: even when life feels like a dumpster fire, God's goodness always prevails.

I'm reminded of the remarkable story of Immaculée Ilibagiza, a survivor of the Rwandan genocide. In 1994, Immaculée and seven other women spent 91 days huddled silently in a tiny bathroom, hiding from the killers who were hunting them. She lost most of her family during this horrific time.

Yet, in the midst of this unimaginable horror, Immaculée experienced God's goodness. She found strength in prayer and even learned to forgive those who had caused such devastation. After her ordeal, Immaculée didn't let bitterness consume her. Instead, she chose to share her story of faith, forgiveness, and the prevailing goodness of God.

Immaculée went on to work for the United Nations, write books about her experiences, and become a motivational speaker. Her life stands as a powerful testament to how God's goodness can shine even in the darkest of circumstances.

In my own life, those periods of depression that once felt hopeless? They've given me a deep well of empathy to draw from in counseling others. The career setbacks that seemed like dead ends? They've become doorways to connect with people from all walks of life in my current ministry.

WEEK 2 DAY 3 OF OUR JOURNEY
GOODNESS PREVAILS

God's goodness isn't always about preventing bad things from happening. Sometimes, it's about His faithfulness in bringing good out of even the darkest situations. It's about His presence with us in the valley, His power to redeem our pain, and His promise to never leave us or forsake us.

Reflect and Respond:

- How have you experienced God's goodness in unexpected ways, especially during difficult times?
- In what areas of your life do you need to trust in God's goodness right now?
- How might your current challenges be opportunities to witness and share God's goodness with others?

Action Steps:

1. Start a "Goodness Journal." Each day, write down one way you've seen God's goodness, no matter how small.
2. Choose a verse about God's goodness (like our key verse) to memorize and meditate on this week.
3. Look for an opportunity to be a channel of God's goodness to someone else today. How can you reflect His goodness in your interactions?

Remember, even in the hottest fires, God's goodness prevails. It may not always look like we expect, but it's always present, always working, always refining us into the image of Christ. Trust in His goodness today, for it is a refuge that will never fail.

"God's goodness is the root of all goodness; and our goodness, if we have any, springs out of His goodness." - William Tyndale

WEEK 2 DAY 4 OF OUR JOURNEY
IMPURITIES CONSUMED

Key Verse: *"See, I have refined you, though not as silver; I have tested you in the furnace of affliction."* - Isaiah 48:10 NIV

Alright, let's get real for a moment. We all have impurities in our lives - those habits, attitudes, or patterns that don't reflect Christ. For me, it was people-pleasing and finding my worth in my career achievements. God had to turn up the heat to burn those impurities away (and I don't think for a minute we are done yet).

I'm reminded of the transformative story of John Newton, the 18th-century slave trader turned abolitionist and hymn writer. Newton began his career on slave ships, eventually becoming a ship's captain in the slave trade. His life was marked by moral corruption and a blatant disregard for human dignity.

However, God had a refining process in store for Newton. After nearly dying in a violent storm at sea, Newton began to reflect on his life and actions. This experience, combined with his study of the Bible and Christian literature, led to a gradual but profound transformation.

Through this refining fire, God burned away Newton's callousness, greed, and moral blindness. The process wasn't quick or easy, but over time, Newton not only left the slave trade but became a vocal opponent of slavery. He became a minister and wrote hymns, including the beloved "Amazing Grace," which reflects his personal experience of God's refining work.

In my own journey, it took multiple setbacks and those bouts of depression for God to refine away my tendency to find worth in achievements rather than in Him. Each struggle became an opportunity for God to burn away the dross and reveal more of His image in me. (Oh and still working on it...)

IMPURITIES CONSUMED

God's refining process isn't about making us miserable – it's about making us holy. It's about burning away everything that doesn't look like Christ so that we can more clearly reflect His image to the world.

Reflect and Respond:

- What impurities is God working to consume in your life right now?
- How have you seen God refine your character through difficult experiences?

Action Steps:

1. Prayerfully ask God to reveal any impurities in your life that need refining. Write them down and surrender them to Him.
2. Share with a trusted accountability partner about an area where you're seeking growth. Ask for their prayers and support.
3. Choose one "impurity" to focus on this week. Each day, take a small step towards change in this area.

Remember, beloved, the refiner's fire isn't meant to destroy us – it's meant to purify us. And while it might not always feel like it in the moment, the end result is always worth it. After all, I'd rather be gold tested by fire than fool's gold any day of the week!

"The Word of God is like a lion. You don't have to defend a lion. All you have to do is let the lion loose, and the lion will defend itself." - Charles Spurgeon

CHRIST'S IMAGE

Key Verse: *"And we all, who with unveiled faces contemplate the Lord's glory, are being transformed into his image with ever-increasing glory, which comes from the Lord, who is the Spirit."* - 2 Corinthians 3:18 NIV

You know, friends, in all my career changes and life adventures, I've tried on a lot of different "images." Firefighter, animator, counselor - you name it, I've probably given it a shot. But here's the thing: the only image that really matters is Christ's.

I'm reminded of the powerful transformation in the life of Rosaria Butterfield. Rosaria was a tenured professor of English and women's studies at Syracuse University, and a committed LGBT activist. She was also an outspoken critic of Christianity.

But God had other plans. Through an unlikely friendship with a local pastor and his wife, Rosaria began to study the Bible, initially to argue against it. However, as she read, she found herself increasingly drawn to the person of Jesus Christ.

Over time, Rosaria's image began to change. Her identity, once rooted in her sexuality and academic achievements, was gradually transformed as she embraced Christ. It wasn't an easy or quick process, but slowly, the image of Christ began to shine through her.

Today, Rosaria is a committed Christian, author, and speaker. She's known for her compassionate approach to controversial issues, embodying Christ's love while standing firm in biblical truth. Her story is a testament to the power of Christ to transform us into His image, no matter where we start.

In my own life, I've had to learn (and relearn) that true transformation isn't about trying harder or doing more. It's about spending time in God's presence, allowing His Spirit to change us from the inside out.

CHRIST'S IMAGE

Becoming like Christ isn't a self-help project. It's a surrender. It's allowing God to chip away everything that doesn't look like Jesus, even when that process is uncomfortable or challenging.

Reflect and Respond:

- ·In what ways have you seen yourself becoming more like Christ through your trials?
- ·What aspects of Christ's character do you most want to see developed in your life?

Action Steps:
1. Choose one characteristic of Jesus (love, patience, compassion, etc.) to focus on this week. Look for opportunities to practice this trait daily.
2. Find a picture or artwork depicting Jesus that resonates with you. Spend time in prayer, asking God to shape you more into His image as you contemplate the image.
3. Share with a friend or family member how you've seen God changing you to be more like Christ. Ask them to pray for your continued transformation.

Remember, we're not just trying to be better versions of ourselves. We're being transformed into the image of Christ. It's a lifelong process, but it's the most important journey we'll ever undertake. So let's keep our eyes fixed on Jesus, trusting that He who began this good work in us will be faithful to complete it.

"The Christian life is not about finding your true self, but losing yourself in order to find yourself in Christ." - Timothy Keller

REFINED REFLECTION

Key Verse: *"But we have this treasure in jars of clay to show that this all-surpassing power is from God and not from us." - 2 Corinthians 4:7 NIV*

As we near the end of our week focusing on the refining fire, it's important to remember that the goal isn't perfection, but reflection. God isn't expecting us to become flawless; He's inviting us to become faithful reflections of His grace and power.

Charles Spurgeon, the renowned 19th-century Baptist preacher, also struggled with severe depression throughout his life. Despite his immense talent and influence, Spurgeon's mental health battles often made him question his ability to minister effectively. How could he guide others when he himself felt so broken?

But as Spurgeon journeyed through his own refining fire, he began to see how God was using his struggles to shape him into a powerful instrument of His grace. His experiences with depression didn't disqualify him from ministry - they equipped him with a unique empathy and understanding for those facing similar battles.

Spurgeon came to embody the truth of today's verse. He was indeed a jar of clay - cracked, imperfect, and sometimes fragile. But it was through those very cracks that God's light shone most brightly. His vulnerability became a conduit for God's strength. His openness about his struggles allowed others to see the treasure of God's grace at work in his life.

This truth is also beautifully illustrated in the life of the Apostle Paul. Despite his "thorn in the flesh" - a persistent ailment that tormented him - Paul learned that God's power was made perfect in his weakness (2 Corinthians 12:9). His physical limitations became the very means through which God's strength was displayed.

REFINED REFLECTION

Being refined doesn't mean becoming a perfect, unblemished vessel. It means becoming a transparent one - a life through which others can clearly see God's power and love at work. Spurgeon's ministry touched countless lives not despite his struggles, but often because of them. Paul's impact for the Kingdom was magnified through his weakness.

Reflect and Respond:

- How has God used your weaknesses or struggles to display His strength?
- In what ways might your current challenges be opportunities to reflect God's grace to others?
- How does seeing yourself as a "jar of clay" containing God's treasure change your perspective on your imperfections?

Action Steps:

1. Write a letter to God, acknowledging your "cracks" and inviting Him to shine His light through them.
2. Meditate on 2 Corinthians 4:7-10. How does this passage encourage you in your current circumstances?
3. Look for opportunities today to be transparent about your challenges and God's faithfulness. Allow others to see the "treasure" within your "jar of clay."

Remember, the refining process isn't about making us shinier on the outside. It's about making us more transparent so that the light of Christ within us can shine more brightly to a world in need. Embrace your status as a jar of clay, and let God's power be seen through your life.

ENDURING GOLD

Key Verse: *"These have come so that the proven genuineness of your faith—of greater worth than gold, which perishes even though refined by fire—may result in praise, glory and honor when Jesus Christ is revealed."* - 1 Peter 1:7 NIV

As we conclude our week on the refining fire, let's reflect on the enduring nature of refined faith. Peter tells us that our faith, when tested and proven genuine, is of greater worth than gold. That's a powerful statement, considering how valuable gold is in our world.

Remember Horatio Spafford, the 19th-century American lawyer and hymnwriter? Spafford had built a successful law practice in Chicago and invested heavily in real estate. He seemed to have it all. But when the Great Chicago Fire of 1871 hit, he lost a fortune. His gold, so to speak, perished in the fire of financial crisis.

Just two years later, Spafford faced an even greater tragedy. His four daughters drowned in a shipwreck while crossing the Atlantic Ocean. In the midst of this unimaginable loss, something remarkable happened. The faith that had been quietly growing beneath the surface of his success suddenly came to the forefront. As his material wealth and earthly joy diminished, the true gold of his faith began to shine.

Spafford's trust in God didn't waver in the face of financial ruin and personal tragedy. Instead, it deepened. His response to these trials was to pen the hymn "It Is Well With My Soul," a powerful testimony of faith in the midst of suffering. His joy, once perhaps tied to his success and family life, now flowed from a deeper source - his unshakeable relationship with God.

You see, the fire that consumed Spafford's worldly gold refined and revealed the true gold of his faith. And this faith - tested, tried, and proven genuine - was of far greater worth than any material wealth or earthly comfort he had lost.

This echoes the experience of Job in the Bible. Despite losing his wealth, his children, and his health, Job's faith endured. He declared, "*Though he slay me, yet will I hope in him*" (Job 13:15). His refined faith shone brighter than any worldly possessions he had lost.

Reflect and Respond:

- How has your faith been tested recently? In what ways has it emerged stronger?
- What "gold" in your life might God be asking you to hold loosely, in order to refine the gold of your faith?
- How does knowing your refined faith is "of greater worth than gold" change your perspective on trials?

Action Steps:

1. Reflect on your journey through this week's devotions. Write down three ways you've seen God refining your faith.
2. Choose a "refining verse" (like our key verse or another that has spoken to you this week) to carry with you into the challenges ahead.
3. Spend time in prayer, thanking God for His refining work in your life and asking for strength to endure future trials.

As we close this week, remember that the refining process is ongoing. There will be more fires, more challenges, more opportunities for your faith to be proven genuine. But take heart - each trial is an opportunity for your faith to shine more brightly, to become more precious, to bring more glory to God

"*Count it all joy, my brothers, when you meet trials of various kinds, for you know that the testing of your faith produces steadfastness.*" - James 1:2-3 ESV

YOUR JOURNAL

My Notes

_____

_____

_____

_____

_____

_____

_____

_____

_____

_____

_____

_____

_____

_____

_____

_____

_____

_____

_____

_____

_____

_____

_____

_____

_____

_____

Dear friend,

As we emerge from this week focused on the refining fire, I pray you're feeling not scorched, but refined. The heat you've endured isn't meant to destroy you, but to purify and strengthen you.

In the days ahead, when you face challenges, remember that you're in the hands of the Master Refiner. He knows exactly how much heat you need and for how long. Trust His process, even when you can't see the end result.

Look for the gold that's emerging in your life - the patience, perseverance, and character being formed in you. And remember, just as gold reflects the image of the refiner, you are being transformed more and more into the image of Christ.

May you walk forward with confidence, knowing that the God who began a good work in you will carry it on to completion.

Shine on, Doug

WEEK 3
COMPASSION'S CALL

Embracing God's Heart in a Hurting World

WEEK 3 DAY 1 OF OUR JOURNEY
EMPATHY'S GROWTH

Key Verse: *"Rejoice with those who rejoice; mourn with those who mourn."* - Romans 12:15 NIV

You know, friends, there was a time in my life when I thought I had empathy all figured out. After all, I'd been through my share of ups and downs - from career changes to battles with depression. I figured that made me an expert in understanding others' pain. But let me tell you, God has a way of expanding our capacity for empathy in ways we never expected.

Take the story of Job's friends, for instance. When they first heard about Job's suffering, they did something remarkable - they sat with him in silence for seven days and nights (Job 2:13). That's empathy at its finest. But then, well, they opened their mouths. They started offering explanations and advice, trying to fix Job's situation. Sound familiar? I've been there, done that, and probably printed the t-shirt.

You see, true empathy isn't about having all the answers or even about having gone through the exact same experience. It's about being willing to enter into someone else's pain, to sit with them in the ashes without trying to sweep them away.

I'm reminded of the story of Brennan Manning, author of "The Ragamuffin Gospel." Manning, a recovering alcoholic, and ex Franciscan monk once shared how he relapsed after years of sobriety. He expected judgment and condemnation from his Christian friends. Instead, one of them simply said, "Me too," and shared his own struggle with sin. That's empathy in action - it doesn't minimize the pain or the sin, but it reminds us we're not alone in our brokenness.

I've always been fascinated by people's unique stories. But God has been teaching me that true empathy goes beyond fascination. It requires us to be fully present, to listen without judgment, and to resist the urge to "fix" everything.

EMPATHY'S GROWTH

Empathy's growth often happens in uncomfortable places. It's in the hospital waiting room, the funeral home, or sitting across from someone whose life is falling apart. It's in those moments when we don't know what to say, so we simply say, "I'm here. I'm with you."

As we grow in empathy, we become more like Jesus, who was moved with compassion when He saw the crowds (Matthew 9:36). He didn't just observe their pain from a distance - He entered into it, ultimately taking it upon Himself on the cross.

Reflect and Respond:

- When have you experienced true empathy from someone else? How did it impact you?
- In what areas of your life is God calling you to grow in empathy?

Action Steps:

1. Practice active listening this week. When someone shares a struggle, resist the urge to offer advice. Instead, try saying, "That sounds really difficult. How are you feeling about that?"
2. Reach out to someone who's going through a tough time. Don't wait for them to ask for help - take the initiative to be present with them in their pain.
3. Reflect on a past situation where you could have shown more empathy. What would you do differently now? Use this reflection to inform your future interactions.

Remember, growing in empathy isn't always comfortable, but it's always worthwhile. As we open our hearts to others' pain, we become more effective channels of God's love and grace. And in the end, isn't that what we're all called to be?

COMFORT'S OVERFLOW

Key Verse: *"Praise be to the God and Father of our Lord Jesus Christ, the Father of compassion and the God of all comfort, who comforts us in all our troubles, so that we can comfort those in any trouble with the comfort we ourselves receive from God."* - 2 Corinthians 1:3-4 NIV

You know, there was a time in my life when I thought my struggles were just that - my struggles. Those bouts of depression, the career chaos, the times I felt like I was drowning in anxiety? I figured they were just obstacles to overcome, chapters to close and move on from. But oh, how God has a way of repurposing our pain!

Think about Joseph in the Bible. Talk about a guy who had every right to be bitter! Sold into slavery by his own brothers, falsely accused, thrown into prison - it's like a soap opera, but with sandals. Yet, years later, when he finally faced his brothers again, he said something profound: *"You intended to harm me, but God intended it for good to accomplish what is now being done, the saving of many lives"* (Genesis 50:20). Joseph's pain became the very tool God used to save not just his family, but an entire nation.

Now, I'm no Joseph (though I did have a colorful coat phase in the '80s), but I've seen God work in similar ways in my own life. Those struggles with depression that once left me feeling helpless? They've become a wellspring of empathy in my counseling ministry. The career rollercoaster that made me feel like a failure? It's given me a unique ability to connect with people from all walks of life.

The story of Corrie ten Boom, a Dutch Christian who, along with her family, helped many Jews escape the Nazi Holocaust during World War II. She was eventually arrested and sent to a concentration camp, where she endured unimaginable suffering. After the war, Corrie could have been consumed by bitterness and trauma. Instead, she traveled the world sharing her story and the message of God's forgiveness and love. Her experiences of God's comfort in the midst of extreme adversity became a source of comfort for countless others.

COMFORT'S OVERFLOW

You see, comfort isn't meant to be a dead end – it's meant to be a throughway. God comforts us not just to make us feel better, but to make us better comforters. It's like a divine game of "Pay It Forward," where our experiences of God's comfort equip us to extend that same comfort to others.

I've always enjoyed connecting with people, but there's a depth of connection that only comes when we're willing to be vulnerable about our own struggles and the comfort we've received. It's in those moments of shared vulnerability that God's comfort truly overflows.

Reflect and Respond:

- How have your past struggles equipped you to comfort others?
- In what areas of your life do you need to receive God's comfort right now?

Action Steps:

1. Write a letter to your younger self, sharing how God has used your struggles for good. Keep this letter as a reminder of God's faithfulness.
2. Identify someone in your life who's going through a struggle similar to one you've faced. Reach out to them this week and share your story of how God comforted you.
3. Start a "Comfort Journal." Each day, write down one way you've experienced God's comfort and one way you've had the opportunity to extend comfort to others.

Remember, our comfort isn't meant to be hoarded – it's meant to be shared. As we allow God's comfort to overflow from our lives into the lives of others, we become living testimonies of His grace and love. And in a world that's hurting, there's no greater calling than that.

SHARED TEARS

Key Verse: *"Jesus wept."* - John 11:35 NIV

You know, friends, in all my years of ministry, I've discovered something profound: sometimes, the most powerful thing we can do is simply weep with those who weep. It's not about having the right words or fixing the problem. It's about being present in the pain.

I remember a time when I was at the lowest point of one of my depressive episodes. A friend came over, and instead of offering advice or trying to cheer me up, he simply sat with me. When I started to cry, he lowered his head, felt the pain, and was just there. In that moment, I felt seen, understood, and less alone. It was a turning point in my journey.

This reminds me of the shortest verse in the Bible: "Jesus wept." Here's the context: Jesus had just arrived in Bethany after his friend Lazarus had died. He knew he was about to perform a miracle and raise Lazarus from the dead. Yet, when he saw Mary and the others weeping, he was deeply moved and began to weep himself (John 11:33-35).

Now, why would Jesus weep if he knew he was about to fix the situation? I believe it's because he understood the power of shared sorrow. He entered fully into the grief of his friends, demonstrating a compassion that goes beyond mere problem-solving.

This idea of shared tears isn't just a New Testament concept. In the book of Job, when Job's friends first arrived and saw his suffering, they "began to weep aloud, and they tore their robes and sprinkled dust on their heads. Then they sat on the ground with him for seven days and seven nights. No one said a word to him, because they saw how great his suffering was" (Job 2:12-13). It was only when they started trying to explain and fix things that they went wrong.

WEEK 3 DAY 3 OF OUR JOURNEY
SHARED TEARS

In our modern world, we often struggle with this concept. We want to fix, to solve, to move on quickly from pain. But there's a holy space in shared sorrow that we shouldn't rush past.

William Sloane Coffin, a prominent Christian minister and activist. When his son died in a car accident, a well-meaning friend said, "I just don't understand the will of God." Coffin replied, "I'll tell you what the will of God is. The will of God is not that young men die in automobile accidents. The will of God is that we love one another and care for each other in our grief."

Truly honoring those stories sometimes means simply being present in their darkest chapters, sharing in their tears without trying to write a happier ending prematurely.

Reflect and Respond:

- When have you experienced the power of someone sharing in your sorrow?
- How comfortable are you with sitting in others' pain without trying to fix it?
-

Action Steps:

1. Practice the ministry of presence this week. When someone shares a struggle, resist the urge to offer solutions. Instead, try saying, "I'm so sorry. This must be really hard for you."
2. Reflect on a time when you rushed to "fix" someone's pain instead of just being present. How might you approach a similar situation differently now?
3. Reach out to someone who's grieving or struggling. Offer to simply sit with them, even in silence if that's what they need.

WOUNDED HEALERS

Key Verse: *"Praise be to the God and Father of our Lord Jesus Christ, the Father of compassion and the God of all comfort, who comforts us in all our troubles, so that we can comfort those in any trouble with the comfort we ourselves receive from God." - 2 Corinthians 1:3-4 NIV*

You know, friends, there was a time when I thought my struggles disqualified me from ministry. Three nervous breakdowns, a revolving door of careers, battles with depression and anxiety - it felt like a resume of failures rather than a platform for helping others. But God, in His infinite wisdom and sometimes questionable sense of humor, had other plans.

I've come to realize that it's often our wounds, our scars, and our struggles that uniquely equip us to minister to others. We become, as Henri Nouwen so beautifully put it, "wounded healers."

Think about the apostle Paul. This guy had a past that would make most of us cringe. He persecuted Christians with a zealous fervor before his dramatic conversion. But it was precisely this background that God used to make Paul one of the most effective ministers of the gospel. His past gave him a unique perspective and a deep well of compassion for those he was trying to reach.

In my own life, those bouts of depression that once left me feeling useless? They've become the very thing that allows me to connect with and counsel others who are walking through the valley of darkness. The career chaos that made me feel like a failure? It's given me a platform to speak hope into the lives of people facing professional uncertainty.

Joni Eareckson Tada, after a diving accident left her quadriplegic at the age of 17, Joni initially fell into deep depression and struggled with her faith. But over time, she allowed God to use her disability as a powerful ministry tool.

WOUNDED HEALERS

Today, she's an internationally known mouth artist, author, and advocate for people with disabilities. Her wound became the source of healing for countless others.

You see, when we minister from our wounds, we're not offering pat answers or cliché platitudes. We're offering authentic, hard-won hope. We're saying, "I've been where you are, and I can testify that God is faithful."

I'm always looking for connections between ideas. And I've come to see that there's a beautiful connection between our wounds and our ability to heal others. It's as if God takes our broken pieces and creates a mosaic of ministry, more beautiful and impactful than we could have imagined.

Reflect and Respond:

- How have your past struggles or current challenges equipped you to help others?
- In what areas of your life might God be calling you to become a "wounded healer"?

Action Steps:

- Write down three of your biggest struggles or wounds. Next to each one, list how God might use that experience to help others.
- Reach out to someone who's going through a struggle similar to one you've faced. Share your story and offer encouragement.
- Start a "Healing Journal." Each day, write down one way you've experienced healing and one way you've had the opportunity to extend healing to others.

Remember, our wounds don't disqualify us from ministry - they often become our most powerful ministry tools.

PURPOSE UNVEILED

Key Verse: *"And we know that in all things God works for the good of those who love him, who have been called according to his purpose."* - Romans 8:28 NIV

You know, friends, if you had told me years ago that my string of career changes, bouts of depression, and moments of doubt would one day be the very things God would use to shape my purpose, I might have laughed. Or cried. Or both. But here we are, and I'm continually amazed at how God weaves our messy threads into His beautiful tapestry.

Think about Joseph in the Bible. Talk about a roller coaster life! Favored son, slave, prisoner, and then second-in-command of Egypt. At any point in that journey, Joseph could have lost sight of God's purpose. But in the end, he was able to say to his brothers, "You intended to harm me, but God intended it for good to accomplish what is now being done, the saving of many lives" (Genesis 50:20). Joseph's purpose was unveiled through his pain.

In my own life, each career change that once felt like a failure has become a unique lens through which I can connect with people from all walks of life. Those struggles with depression that once made me feel useless? They've become the very thing that allows me to speak hope into the lives of others battling mental health challenges. God doesn't waste a thing.

I'm reminded of the story of Nick Vujicic. Born without limbs, Nick struggled with depression and loneliness as a child, even attempting suicide at one point. He questioned his purpose and worth. But as he grew in his faith, he began to see how his unique situation could be used to inspire others.

Today, Nick is a world-renowned motivational speaker, author, and evangelist. He's spoken to millions of people across the globe, offering hope and demonstrating that life without limbs can be limitless. His physical limitations, which once seemed to restrict his purpose, became the very platform God used to unveil his true calling.

PURPOSE UNVEILED

Sometimes it's only in looking back that we can see how God has been weaving together our experiences, our struggles, and even our failures into something beautiful and purposeful.

I often find myself looking for patterns and connections. And I've come to see that there's often a divine strategy behind our seeming detours and setbacks. What looks like a roadblock might actually be a redirect towards our true purpose.

Reflect and Respond:

- Looking back, how have seemingly negative experiences in your life contributed to your current purpose or ministry?
- In what current struggle might God be unveiling a new aspect of your purpose?

Action Steps:

1. Create a timeline of your life, marking significant events - both positive and negative. Next to each event, write how God has used or might use that experience for His purpose.
2. Spend time in prayer, asking God to reveal more of His purpose for your life. Be open to unexpected answers!
3. Share your story of how God has revealed purpose through struggle with someone who's currently facing difficulties. Your testimony could be the encouragement they need.

Remember, your purpose is not just despite your struggles, but often because of them. As we surrender our plans to God, He unveils a purpose far greater than we could have imagined. So keep your eyes open, your heart willing, and watch in wonder as God's purpose for your life continues to unfold.

MINISTRY'S BIRTH

Key Verse: *"But he said to me, 'My grace is sufficient for you, for my power is made perfect in weakness.' Therefore I will boast all the more gladly about my weaknesses, so that Christ's power may rest on me."* - 2 Corinthians 12:9 NIV

You know, when I was younger, I had this idea that ministry was for the spiritual elite - those super-Christians who had it all together and never struggled. I couldn't have been more wrong. Looking back now, I can see how God was using every twist and turn of my messy journey to prepare me for the work He had in store.

Those years of career hopping? They gave me a unique ability to relate to people from all walks of life. The battles with depression? They became a wellspring of empathy for those struggling with mental health. Even my nervous breakdowns, as painful as they were, equipped me with firsthand knowledge of God's sustaining grace in our darkest moments. It's as if God took the broken pieces of my life and created a mosaic of ministry opportunities I never could have imagined.

Think about Moses for a moment. Here's a guy who started out as a prince, became a fugitive, and then spent 40 years as a shepherd before God called him to lead the Israelites out of Egypt. Moses didn't feel qualified - he even tried to talk God out of the job! But it was precisely his experiences, even his weaknesses (like his speech impediment), that God used to shape him into the leader Israel needed.

In my own life, each career change that once felt like a failure has become a unique way to relate to people from all walks of life. Those bouts of depression that once left me feeling hopeless? They've become the very thing that allows me to offer hope to others battling mental health challenges. Even my struggles with people-pleasing have given me insight into helping others find their identity in Christ rather than in others' approval.

MINISTRY'S BIRTH

I don't know if you remember the story of Charles Colson. Once known as President Nixon's "hatchet man" during the Watergate scandal, Colson's political career ended in disgrace and a prison sentence. But it was in prison that Colson came to faith in Christ, and out of that experience, Prison Fellowship was born - a ministry that has touched countless lives of inmates and their families around the world.

You see, ministry often isn't born in comfort or success, but in the crucible of our challenges and failures. It's in those places of weakness that we experience God's strength in profound ways, and that experience becomes the foundation of our ministry to others.

Reflect and Respond:

- How have your struggles or weaknesses become a source of ministry to others?
- What current challenge might God be using to birth a new area of ministry in your life?

Action Steps:

1. Write out your testimony, focusing on how God has worked through your weaknesses and struggles. Practice sharing it with a trusted friend.
2. Identify a struggle you're currently facing. Pray about how God might use this experience as a ministry opportunity in the future.
3. Look for an opportunity this week to encourage someone who's going through a similar struggle to one you've faced. Share how God worked in your situation.

Remember, our greatest ministries often arise from our deepest pain. As we surrender our weaknesses to God, He transforms them into powerful tools for His kingdom. So don't despise your struggles - they might just be the birthplace of your most impactful ministry.

SCARS' TESTIMONY

Key Verse: *"I want to know Christ—yes, to know the power of his resurrection and participation in his sufferings, becoming like him in his death"* - Philippians 3:10 NIV

Well, folks, we've come to the end of our week on Compassion's Call, and I can't think of a more fitting topic to close with than the testimony of our scars. You know, for years, I tried to hide my scars - the marks left behind. I thought they made me weak, disqualified me from ministry. But oh, how wrong I was!

Think about the apostle Paul for a moment. This guy had plenty of scars, both physical and emotional. He was beaten, stoned, shipwrecked, and imprisoned. But instead of hiding these scars, Paul boasted in them. Why? Because they were evidence of his participation in Christ's sufferings, proof of God's sustaining grace.

In my own life, I've come to see my scars in a new light. Those periods of depression? They've given me a deep well of empathy for others struggling with mental health. The career changes that once felt like failures? They've become bridges to connect with people from all walks of life. Even the scars from my people-pleasing tendencies have become powerful object lessons in finding our identity in Christ alone.

Have you ever heard the story of Louie Zamperini, whose life is chronicled in the book "Unbroken?" Zamperini survived unimaginable hardships as a POW in World War II, and afterward struggled with PTSD and alcoholism. But when he came to Christ, those scars became a powerful testimony. He even returned to Japan to forgive his former captors, demonstrating the transformative power of God's love.

You see, our scars tell a story - not just of our suffering, but of God's faithfulness through it all. They're not blemishes to be hidden, but badges of honor that testify to God's sustaining grace and transformative power.

SCARS' TESTIMONY

I've found that the deepest connections often come when we're vulnerable about our scars. It's in those moments of shared brokenness that we can point to the healing power of Christ.

Reflect and Respond:

- What scars (emotional, physical, or spiritual) do you carry? How might God use these as a testimony of His grace?
- How has your perspective on your past struggles changed over time?

Action Steps:

1. Write a letter to God, thanking Him for His faithfulness through your past struggles. Be specific about how He's used your scars for good.
2. Share the story of one of your scars with a trusted friend or small group. Focus on how God has worked through that experience.
3. Look for an opportunity this week to encourage someone who's struggling. Use your own scars as a testimony to God's healing and transformative power.

Remember, our scars are sacred. They tell the story of where we've been, but more importantly, they testify to the God who has brought us through. So let's not hide our scars, but hold them out as evidence of God's amazing grace. After all, it was by His wounds that we are healed, and it's often through our wounds that He brings healing to others.

YOUR JOURNAL

My Notes

_____
_____
_____
_____
_____
_____
_____
_____
_____
_____
_____
_____
_____
_____
_____
_____
_____
_____
_____
_____
_____
_____
_____
_____
_____
_____
_____

Dear Friend,

As we conclude this week on answering compassion's call, I hope you've discovered new depths of empathy within yourself. Your experiences - both painful and joyful - have uniquely equipped you to understand and support others.

In the coming days, I encourage you to look for opportunities to extend the comfort you've received. Your scars, your struggles, your victories - all of these can become bridges of understanding to those around you.

Remember, compassion isn't just a feeling; it's an action. Let your empathy move you to make a difference in someone's life, no matter how small it might seem.

May you be filled with the compassion of Christ, allowing His love to flow through you to a world in need.

With a heart full of compassion, Doug

WEEK 4

ETERNAL
PERSPECTIVE

*VIEWING LIFE'S CHALLENGES THROUGH
HEAVEN'S LENS*

TEMPORAL TRIALS

Key Verse: *"For our light and momentary troubles are achieving for us an eternal glory that far outweighs them all."* - 2 Corinthians 4:17 NIV

You know, there were times in my life when my troubles felt anything but light and momentary. Those bouts of depression? They felt like endless dark tunnels. The career setbacks? They seemed like permanent failures. But God has a way of reframing our perspective, doesn't He?

Think about Paul, the guy who wrote our key verse. This wasn't some armchair theologian spouting platitudes. Paul had been beaten, shipwrecked, imprisoned - you name it, he'd been through it. Yet he had the audacity to call these trials "light and momentary." Why? Because he was viewing them through the lens of eternity.

In my own journey, I've had to learn (and relearn) this lesson countless times. When I was in the throes of a nervous breakdown, it felt like my world was ending. But looking back now, I can see how God used that experience to shape me, to prepare me for the ministry He had in store. What seemed like an ending was actually a beginning.

Richard Wurmbrand, was a Romanian minister who spent 14 years in Communist prisons because of his faith. He endured unimaginable torture and isolation. Yet in his book, "Tortured for Christ," he writes about how he and other prisoners would tap messages of encouragement to each other through the walls. They found joy and purpose even in the darkest of circumstances because they were focused on eternity.

It reminds me of mosaics in a church. Up close, each tile looked rough and insignificant. Some are even broken or oddly shaped. But when you step back, you can see the beautiful image they form together. Our trials are like those tiles - they might seem random or purposeless up close, but from an eternal perspective, they're part of a masterpiece God is creating.

TEMPORAL TRIALS

There's often a divine strategy behind our trials - a strategy that's focused on eternity rather than just the here and now.

Reflect and Respond:

- How might your current struggles look different if viewed through the lens of eternity?
- In what ways have past trials prepared you for your current purpose or ministry?

Action Steps:

1. Write down your current biggest challenge. Next to it, write "This too shall pass" as a reminder of its temporal nature.
2. Spend time in prayer, asking God to help you see your trials from His eternal perspective. Journal any insights you receive.
3. Share with a friend how a past trial has shaped you for the better. Encourage each other to keep an eternal perspective.

Remember, our troubles are temporary, but their impact on our character and our eternity is lasting. So let's lift our eyes above our circumstances and fix them on the eternal glory that awaits. After all, the best is yet to come!

ETERNAL HOPE

Key Verse: *"I consider that our present sufferings are not worth comparing with the glory that will be revealed in us."* - Romans 8:18 NIV

Well, folks, if you're anything like me, there have been times when the "present sufferings" felt pretty darn significant. Those nights when depression had me in its grip, or when another career change occurred - they felt like more than I could bear. But Paul's words here challenge us to a radical shift in perspective.

Consider Job for a moment. This guy lost everything - his wealth, his health, his children. His suffering was immense. Yet in the midst of it all, he declared, "*I know that my redeemer lives, and that in the end he will stand on the earth*" (Job 19:25). Job had his eyes fixed on an eternal hope that transcended his present circumstances.

In my own life, I've had to learn to cultivate this eternal hope. When I was going through my third nervous breakdown, it felt like my world was collapsing. But clinging to the promise of God's eternal purposes helped me to keep putting one foot in front of the other. What seemed like an end became a transformative beginning in my journey of faith and ministry.

A good example of this is Brother Yun, a Chinese Christian leader who endured severe persecution for his faith. In his book "The Heavenly Man," he recounts how, even in prison and under torture, the hope of eternity sustained him. He writes, "The worse our situation became, the more we relied on God and the more He revealed His power among us."

You see, eternal hope isn't about denying our present realities. It's about seeing them in light of a greater reality. It's about trusting that God is working out His purposes, even when we can't see or understand them.

ETERNAL HOPE

I've come to see that there's a beautiful connection between our present sufferings and our future glory. Each trial, each struggle, is like a brushstroke in the masterpiece God is creating - a masterpiece that will only be fully revealed in eternity.

Reflect and Respond:

- How does the promise of future glory change your perspective on your current struggles?
- In what areas of your life do you need to cultivate a more eternal perspective?

Action Steps:
1. Create a "Glory Board" - a visual representation of the eternal hope you have in Christ. This could be a collage, a painting, or even a Pinterest board.
2. Memorize Romans 8:18. Recite it to yourself whenever you're facing a particularly difficult situation.
3. Share your eternal hope with someone who's struggling. Sometimes, we all need a reminder to lift our eyes above our circumstances.

Remember, our hope isn't just for some distant future. It's a present reality that can transform how we live today. So, let's anchor ourselves in this eternal hope, allowing it to infuse every aspect of our lives with purpose and joy. After all, the best is not just yet to come - it's already begun in Christ!

GLORY'S PURSUIT

Key Verse: *"So we fix our eyes not on what is seen, but on what is unseen, since what is seen is temporary, but what is unseen is eternal."* - 2 Corinthians 4:18 NIV

You know, there was a time in my life when I was fixated on the "seen" things - career success, financial stability, the approval of others. I was chasing after what I thought would bring me glory. But let me tell you, God had a different kind of glory in mind for me.

Remember Moses for a moment. Here's a guy who had it all in Egypt - power, prestige, palace living. But he gave it all up to lead a bunch of complaining Israelites through the desert. Why? Because he was "looking ahead to his reward" (Hebrews 11:26). Moses was in pursuit of a glory that transcended the temporary glories of this world.

In my own journey, it took a lot, for me to start shifting my gaze from the seen to the unseen. Each setback, each struggle, became an invitation to look beyond my circumstances and fix my eyes on eternal realities.

There is a powerful story of Jim Elliot, the missionary who was killed while trying to reach the Auca Indians in Ecuador. Before his death, he wrote in his journal, "He is no fool who gives what he cannot keep to gain that which he cannot lose." Man, I love that quote! Jim understood that true glory isn't found in preserving our lives or pursuing worldly success, but in sacrificing ourselves for the eternal purposes of God.

You see, pursuing God's glory often looks foolish by the world's standards. It might mean choosing a lower-paying job that allows you to serve others. It might mean facing ridicule for standing up for your faith. It might mean loving the unlovable or forgiving the unforgivable. But these "foolish" choices are actually investments in eternity.

GLORY'S PURSUIT

I suppose, one of the most clear lessons I've learned is that sometimes, the most important action is to pause, refocus, and realign my pursuits with God's eternal purposes.

Reflect and Respond:

- What "seen" things are you currently fixated on that might be distracting you from eternal realities?
- How might your decisions change if you were more focused on the "unseen" eternal things?

Action Steps:

1. Take an "eternal inventory" of your life. List out your activities, relationships, and goals. Next to each, write how it connects to eternal purposes.
2. Practice "eternity spotting" this week. Each day, try to identify one way you see God's eternal purposes at work in your everyday life.
3. Choose one "seen" thing you've been pursuing and intentionally surrender it to God. Ask Him to help you pursue His glory instead.

Remember, we're not just living for the here and now. We're living for eternity. So, let's lift our eyes above the temporary glories of this world and fix them on the eternal glory that awaits us in Christ. That's a pursuit that will never disappoint!

JOY'S FOUNDATION

Key Verse: *"Though you have not seen him, you love him; and even though you do not see him now, you believe in him and are filled with an inexpressible and glorious joy"* - 1 Peter 1:8 NIV

Listen, there have been times when joy felt about as attainable as climbing Mount Everest in flip-flops. Those dark nights of depression, the sting of career setbacks, the weight of anxiety - they can all conspire to rob us of joy. But Peter here is talking about a joy that's different, a joy that's not dependent on our circumstances.

Consider the example of Paul and Silas in Acts 16. These guys were beaten, thrown into prison, their feet fastened in stocks. Not exactly a Hallmark moment, right? But what do we find them doing? Singing hymns and praying at midnight! They had tapped into a source of joy that transcended their dire circumstances.

In my own life, I've had to learn (and relearn) that true joy isn't found in the absence of trouble, but in the presence of Christ. During one particularly rough patch of depression, I remember crying out to God, feeling totally joyless. It was then that I began to understand - joy isn't a feeling to chase, it's a Person to embrace.

I'm reminded of the story of Eric Liddell, the Olympic runner turned missionary, whose life inspired the film "Chariots of Fire." When faced with the choice between competing on Sunday (which he believed dishonored God) and possibly winning an Olympic medal, he chose to honor God. He famously said, "God made me fast. And when I run, I feel His pleasure." Liddell understood that true joy comes from aligning our lives with God's purposes, not from worldly success or acclaim.

You see, joy founded on Christ is unshakeable because Christ Himself is unshakeable. It's not about plastering on a happy face or denying our struggles. It's about finding our ultimate satisfaction and delight in a relationship with Jesus, come what may.

JOY'S FOUNDATION

I've found that the deepest, most joy-filled connections come when we're anchored in Christ together, encouraging each other to keep our eyes on Him.

Reflect and Respond:

- Where are you currently looking for joy? How might focusing more on your relationship with Christ change your perspective?
- Can you recall a time when you experienced joy even in difficult circumstances? What made that possible?

Action Steps:

1. Start a "Joy Journal." Each day, write down one way you've experienced joy in Christ, especially in the midst of challenges.
2. Choose a "joy verse" to memorize and meditate on this week. Let it be an anchor for your soul when circumstances threaten to steal your joy.
3. Reach out to someone who's struggling and share how Christ has been the source of your joy. Offer to pray with them.

Remember, our joy isn't dependent on what happens to us, but on who holds us. So, let's anchor ourselves firmly in Christ, allowing His joy to become our strength, no matter what storms may come our way. After all, with Jesus as our foundation, we have reason for "inexpressible and glorious joy" every single day!

SUFFERING'S PURPOSE

Key Verse: *"Not only so, but we also glory in our sufferings, because we know that suffering produces perseverance; perseverance, character; and character, hope."* - Romans 5:3-4 NIV

Alright, friends, let's be real for a moment. When we're in the thick of suffering, "glorying" in it is probably the last thing on our minds. I remember times finding purpose in my pain seemed about as likely as finding a snowball in the Sahara.

But Paul here is presenting a radical perspective on suffering. He's not saying we should enjoy suffering (let's not get crazy here), but that we can see purpose in it. It's like spiritual weight training - the resistance builds our spiritual muscles.

Think about Joseph in the Old Testament. This guy went through the wringer - sold into slavery by his own brothers, falsely accused, thrown into prison. But years later, he was able to say to those same brothers, "You intended to harm me, but God intended it for good" (Genesis 50:20). Joseph saw the purpose behind his suffering.

In my own journey, those periods of depression that once felt purposeless? They've given me a deep well of empathy to draw from in counseling others. The career setbacks that seemed like dead ends? They've become doorways to connect with people from all walks of life in my current ministry.

Look at Joni Eareckson Tadas' story. After a diving accident left her quadriplegic, Joni initially struggled to find any purpose in her suffering. But over time, she allowed God to use her experience to minister to millions through her art, writing, and advocacy for people with disabilities. Her suffering became a platform for powerful ministry.

SUFFERING'S PURPOSE

You see, suffering has a way of stripping away the non-essentials and revealing what truly matters. It's like a refiner's fire, burning away the dross and leaving behind pure gold. And in God's economy, nothing is wasted - not even our pain.

I've come to see that our sufferings, and how we respond to them, are a crucial part of our unique testimonies.

Reflect and Respond:

- How have past sufferings shaped your character or deepened your faith?
- In what current struggle might God be producing perseverance, character, or hope in you?

Action Steps:

1. Write a letter to your future self about a current struggle. Include how you hope to see God use this for good in your life and others'.
2. Choose one character trait you'd like to develop (patience, compassion, etc.). Pray for opportunities to grow in this area, even if it involves challenges.
3. Share with someone how a past suffering has ultimately strengthened your faith or character. Offer encouragement to someone going through a similar struggle.

Remember, our sufferings are not random or purposeless. They're opportunities for growth, refinement, and ultimately, hope. So let's not waste our pain, but allow God to use it to shape us more into the image of Christ. After all, it's often in our deepest valleys that we experience our highest growth.

HEAVEN'S ANTICIPATION

Key Verse: *"But our citizenship is in heaven. And we eagerly await a Savior from there, the Lord Jesus Christ."* - Philippians 3:20 NIV

You know, there was a time in my life when the idea of heaven felt about as relevant to my daily life as the price of tea in China. I was so focused on building my little kingdom here on earth - jumping from career to career, chasing after success and significance. But Paul here is reminding us of a profound truth: this world is not our true home.

Think about Abraham in the Old Testament. God called him to leave everything familiar and journey to an unknown land. Hebrews 11:10 tells us that Abraham was looking forward to "the city with foundations, whose architect and builder is God." Abraham lived with a sense of heavenly anticipation.

In my own journey, it took multiple setbacks, bouts of depression, and yes, even those three nervous breakdowns, for me to start lifting my eyes above my earthly circumstances. Each struggle became an invitation to remember that my true citizenship, my real home, is in heaven.

There's a story of Dietrich Bonhoeffer, the German theologian and pastor who resisted the Nazi regime. Even as he faced imprisonment and eventual execution, Bonhoeffer's writings reflect a profound awareness of his heavenly citizenship. In one of his letters from prison, he wrote, "Jesus Christ lived in the midst of his enemies. At the end all his disciples deserted him. On the Cross he was utterly alone, surrounded by evildoers and mockers. For this cause he had come, to bring peace to the enemies of God. So the Christian, too, belongs not in the seclusion of a cloistered life but in the thick of foes."

Bonhoeffer's heavenly perspective allowed him to live with courage and purpose, even in the face of great evil and personal danger. He understood that his ultimate allegiance was not to any earthly kingdom, but to the kingdom of God.

HEAVEN'S ANTICIPATION

You see, when we live with heaven in view, it changes everything. It doesn't mean we become so heavenly minded that we're no earthly good. Rather, it means we live our earthly lives with heavenly purpose. We make decisions based on eternal values, not just temporal ones.

Reflect and Respond:

- How might your priorities or decisions change if you lived with a greater awareness of your heavenly citizenship?
- In what areas of your life do you need to cultivate a more eternal perspective?

Action Steps:

1. Start each day this week by reminding yourself, "My citizenship is in heaven." Notice how it affects your perspective on daily challenges and decisions.
2. Create a "Heaven List" - write down things you're looking forward to about eternity with God. Refer to this list when earthly struggles feel overwhelming.
3. Share with a friend or family member how your hope of heaven impacts your daily life. Encourage each other to live with eternal perspective.

Remember, we're just passing through this world. Our true home awaits us. So let's live each day with joyful anticipation of our heavenly future, allowing that hope to infuse our present with purpose and peace. After all, the best is yet to come!

FOREVER'S EMBRACE

Key Verse: *"He will wipe every tear from their eyes. There will be no more death or mourning or crying or pain, for the old order of things has passed away."* – Revelation 21:4 NIV

Well, friends, we've come to the end of another journey together, and what a fitting verse to close with. You know, there have been times in life when this promise felt almost too good to be true. No more tears? No more pain? It seemed as distant as the stars.

But this verse isn't just pie-in-the-sky wishful thinking. It's a rock-solid promise from the God who keeps His word. It's the grand finale of His redemptive story, the ultimate happy ending that makes all the plot twists and challenges of our earthly lives worthwhile.

Think about John, the writer of Revelation. He was exiled on the island of Patmos, probably wondering if he'd ever see his loved ones again. Yet God gave him this incredible vision of the future – a future where all wrongs are made right, all hurts are healed, and we're finally, fully embraced by our loving Father.

In my own life, this promise has become an anchor for my soul. When I'm counseling someone through grief, or when I'm wrestling with my own pain, I remind myself - and them - that this is not the end of the story. There's a day coming when God Himself will wipe away our tears.

Horatio Spafford, who wrote the hymn "It Is Well With My Soul" after losing his four daughters in a shipwreck, faced unimaginable loss, yet he was able to pen the words, "And Lord, haste the day when my faith shall be sight, the clouds be rolled back as a scroll; the trump shall resound, and the Lord shall descend, even so, it is well with my soul." Spafford was living in light of this eternal promise.

FOREVER'S EMBRACE

This promise of 'forever's embrace' isn't just about a future hope – it changes how we live today. It gives us courage to face our pain, strength to persevere through trials, and joy even in the midst of sorrow. Because we know that this is not all there is.

Reflect and Respond:

- How does the promise of Revelation 21:4 impact how you view your current struggles?
- In what ways can you live today in light of this eternal promise?

Action Steps:

1. Write a letter to yourself from the perspective of your future, perfected self in heaven. What would you want to remind your earthly self about God's faithfulness and the joy to come?
2. Choose a visual reminder of God's promise (a photo, a piece of art, etc.) and place it where you'll see it daily. Let it prompt you to live with eternal perspective.
3. Share the hope of Revelation 21:4 with someone who's hurting. Offer to pray with them, asking God to make this future hope a present comfort.

As we close this journey together, remember, friends, that the God who will one day wipe away every tear is with you right now, in the midst of your joys and sorrows. Let's live each day in light of our eternal hope, allowing the promise of forever's embrace to transform how we face today's challenges. After all, we know how the story ends – and it's more beautiful than we can imagine!

"Therefore encourage one another and build each other up, just as in fact you are doing." - 1 Thessalonians 5:11 NIV

My Notes

EPILOGUE

Dear friend,

As we come to the end of this devotional journey, I want to thank you for allowing me to walk alongside you these past four weeks. We've explored the depths of brokenness, felt the heat of refining fires, answered compassion's call, and glimpsed the eternal perspective that can transform our earthly journey.

Throughout this series, I've shared snippets of my own story - from career changes and health scares to battles with depression and anxiety. But these weren't meant to put the spotlight on me. Rather, they were shared to illustrate a simple yet profound truth: we're all on this journey together, navigating the highs and lows of life, and none of us is alone.

Life is a tapestry of joy and pain, of victories and setbacks. Some days, we feel on top of the world; other days, we struggle to find hope. But in every season, God is present, working all things together for the good of those who love Him.

Remember, your brokenness is not the end of your story - it's often the beginning of God's most beautiful work in your life. The refining fires you face aren't meant to destroy you, but to purify and strengthen you. Your pain can become a wellspring of compassion for others. And every challenge you face is preparing you for an eternal weight of glory that far outweighs them all.

As you move forward from here, I encourage you to:
1. Embrace your brokenness, knowing that God specializes in creating masterpieces from shattered pieces.
2. Trust the refining process, even when the heat feels unbearable.
3. Allow your experiences - both joyful and painful - to cultivate deep compassion for others.
4. Live with an eternal perspective, knowing that your citizenship is in heaven.

EPILOGUE CONTINUED

Above all, remember that you are deeply loved by a God who is intimately involved in every detail of your life. He sees your struggles, bottles your tears, celebrates your victories, and is constantly working to conform you to the image of His Son.

May you walk forward with renewed hope, unshakeable faith, and a deep awareness of God's presence in every step of your journey. And may the peace of God, which transcends all understanding, guard your hearts and minds in Christ Jesus.

With grace and peace,
Doug

P.S. "For I am convinced that neither death nor life, neither angels nor demons, neither the present nor the future, nor any powers, neither height nor depth, nor anything else in all creation, will be able to separate us from the love of God that is in Christ Jesus our Lord." - Romans 8:38-39

AFTERWORD

Coming Soon: Month 5 - "More Than a Feeling"

Are you ready to go beyond the surface and explore what real, lasting love looks like?

Join us for our next Rooted series devotional:

"More Than a Feeling: Cultivating Love That Lasts"

In this powerful 4-week journey, we'll explore:
- The initial spark of attraction
- Building healthy communication
- What a God-centered marriage truly looks like
- The transformative power of selfless love

Don't settle for fleeting emotions. Dive deep into love that stands the test of time.

Rooted in faith. Grounded in love. Growing together.

ABOUT THE AUTHOR

Doug Hamilton is a respected pastor, counselor, radio personality, and now author who has dedicated his life to helping others through a ministry of healing and hope. As a Christian counselor, he draws upon his own personal struggles with depression and anxiety to offer compassionate guidance to individuals and families facing life's challenges.

With a strong focus on fostering healthy communication within families and church communities, Doug provides invaluable insights and practical strategies for building stronger, more resilient relationships. His counseling philosophy is rooted in the belief that open, honest dialogue is the foundation for growth and understanding.

In addition to his work with families and congregations, Doug is passionate about empowering current and future leaders. Through leadership training programs, he equips individuals with the skills and wisdom needed to guide others with integrity, empathy, and a servant's heart.

As a counselor for couples, Doug helps husbands and wives navigate the complexities of marriage, offering a safe space for healing, reconciliation, and renewed commitment. His approach blends biblical principles with proven counseling techniques to help couples build a lasting, and fulfilling union.

ACKNOWLEDGEMENT

In writing "Unshakeable Faith: Finding Strength and Purpose in Life's Broken Places," I've been blessed with support from many people throughout my life's journey.

First and foremost, I thank God for His constant guidance and the strength He provides, especially in life's challenging moments.

To my family and friends, your encouragement and patience throughout this project have been invaluable. Your faith in me kept me going when the path seemed uncertain.

A special thank you goes to Clint Eastman, my youth pastor from decades ago. Clint, though it's been nearly half a century since you were my youth pastor, your example as a Godly, patient, and kind man has left an indelible mark on my life.

The impact you've had on my faith journey is immeasurable, and much of what I've written in these pages reflects the wisdom and grace you showed all those years ago. Your influence has truly stood the test of time.

COMPLETED BOOKS IN THE ROOTED
12 DEVOTIONAL SERIES

WHEN THE GOING GETS TOUGH

RESTORING WHAT WAS BROKEN

TRUSTING GOD IN LIFE'S STORMS

UNSHAKEABLE FAITH

STAY TUNED FOR MORE

This collection of Months is designed to encourage and strengthen believers in their walk with God through all seasons of life. It explores major themes that followers of Jesus had to face as they navigate a broken world while clinging to biblical truths and the hope of eternity.

The Weeks dive into topics like persevering through unrelenting trials and hardship with faith in God's sovereignty, dealing with anxiety and weariness by anchoring to Christ's peace, pursuing reconciliation and unity within broken relationships by His grace, and stewarding practical areas like finances and decision-making by seeking God's wisdom.

Each thematic section features a week-long Week with Scripture reflections and real-life application steps to take God's Word from head to heart. The writer incorporates personal stories with biblical examples of imperfect heroes of faith leaning on God's compassion and power when human strength ran out.

While acknowledging the messy complexities of living in a fallen world, these Weeks point to the one unshakable anchor for our souls - our Shepherd King Jesus who authors our redemption stories. He intimately understands human suffering and guides wanderers to streams of eternal hope rising even from the ashes of crushed dreams or traumatized relationships.

The ultimate aim of this 12 month collection is that fellow travelers discover courage for the journey ahead no matter what giants or storms may assault their faith. By digging deeply into Scripture together, may broken lives find wholeness and purpose.

Made in United States
Orlando, FL
10 August 2024

50232837R00050